RHOYAL WOMEN Get Things Done

TO DO LIST NOTEBOOK

THINGS TO DO:

DATE:

Priority:

THINGS TO DO:

DATE:

Priority:

THINGS TO DO:

DATE:

Priority:

THINGS TO DO:

DATE:

Priority:

THINGS TO DO:

DATE:

Priority:

THINGS TO DO:

DATE:

Priority:

THINGS TO DO:

DATE:

Priority:

THINGS TO DO:

DATE:

Priority:

THINGS TO DO:

DATE:

Priority:

THINGS TO DO:

DATE:

Priority:

THINGS TO DO:

DATE:

Priority:

THINGS TO DO:

DATE:

Priority:

THINGS TO DO:

DATE:

Priority:

THINGS TO DO:

DATE:

Priority:

THINGS TO DO:

DATE:

Priority:

THINGS TO DO:

DATE:

Priority:

THINGS TO DO:

DATE:

Priority:

THINGS TO DO:

DATE:

Priority:

THINGS TO DO:

DATE:

Priority:

THINGS TO DO:

DATE:

Priority:

THINGS TO DO:

DATE:

Priority:

THINGS TO DO:

DATE:

Priority:

THINGS TO DO:

DATE:

Priority:

THINGS TO DO: DATE:

Priority:

THINGS TO DO:

DATE:

Priority:

THINGS TO DO:

DATE:

Priority:

THINGS TO DO:

DATE:

Priority:

THINGS TO DO:

DATE:

Priority:

THINGS TO DO:

DATE:

Priority:

THINGS TO DO:

DATE:

Priority:

THINGS TO DO:

DATE:

- [ ]
- [ ]
- [ ]
- [ ]
- [ ]
- [ ]
- [ ]
- [ ]
- [ ]
- [ ]
- [ ]
- [ ]
- [ ]
- [ ]
- [ ]
- [ ]
- [ ]
- [ ]

- [ ]
- [ ]
- [ ]
- [ ]
- [ ]
- [ ]
- [ ]
- [ ]
- [ ]
- [ ]
- [ ]
- [ ]
- [ ]
- [ ]
- [ ]
- [ ]
- [ ]
- [ ]

Priority:

- [ ]
- [ ]
- [ ]
- [ ]

- [ ]
- [ ]
- [ ]
- [ ]

THINGS TO DO:

DATE:

Priority:

THINGS TO DO:

DATE:

Priority:

THINGS TO DO:

DATE:

Priority:

THINGS TO DO:

DATE:

Priority:

THINGS TO DO:

DATE:

Priority:

THINGS TO DO:

DATE:

Priority:

THINGS TO DO:

DATE:

Priority:

THINGS TO DO:

DATE:

Priority:

THINGS TO DO:

DATE:

Priority:

THINGS TO DO:

DATE:

- [ ]
- [ ]
- [ ]
- [ ]
- [ ]
- [ ]
- [ ]
- [ ]
- [ ]
- [ ]
- [ ]
- [ ]
- [ ]
- [ ]
- [ ]
- [ ]
- [ ]
- [ ]
- [ ]
- [ ]
- [ ]
- [ ]
- [ ]
- [ ]
- [ ]
- [ ]
- [ ]
- [ ]
- [ ]
- [ ]
- [ ]
- [ ]
- [ ]
- [ ]
- [ ]
- [ ]

Priority:

- [ ]
- [ ]
- [ ]
- [ ]
- [ ]
- [ ]
- [ ]
- [ ]

THINGS TO DO:

DATE:

Priority:

THINGS TO DO:

DATE:

Priority:

THINGS TO DO: DATE:

Priority:

THINGS TO DO:

DATE:

Priority:

THINGS TO DO:

DATE:

Priority:

THINGS TO DO:

DATE:

Priority:

THINGS TO DO:

DATE:

Priority:

THINGS TO DO:

DATE:

Priority:

THINGS TO DO:

DATE:

Priority:

THINGS TO DO:

DATE:

Priority:

THINGS TO DO:

DATE:

Priority:

Made in the USA
Las Vegas, NV
02 May 2024

89415666R00066